T·IRISH·
TOASTS

Illustrated by
KAREN BAILEY

First published in the United States 1987 by
Chronicle Books
275 Fifth Street
San Francisco, CA 94103
ISBN: 0-87701-469-8

Illustrations © Karen Bailey, 1987

First published in Ireland by
The Appletree Press Ltd, 1987
ISBN: 0-86281-195-3

Ltd. Printed in China. Typeset in 16/20 pt
Novarese Book by Koinonia Ltd. Origination by
J & P Reprographics. Design and production by
Appletree Press, Ireland.

Acknowledgements

For permission to reproduce copyright material the
following acknowledgements are made: to Irish
Distillers Limited for a selection of ten toasts from
Sláinte (© Irish Distillers Group Limited 1980); to
Brendan Kennelly for 'Saint Brigid's Prayer'; to the
Head of the Department of Irish Folklore, University
College Dublin for Niall Ó Dubhthaigh's story and for
the English translation to the Mercier Press (Irish Life
and Lore, Séamus Ó Catháin, Mercier Press, 1982);
also to Dr. Ó Catháin for translations of the four
toasts on pages 16, 28, 31 and 40 (Irish Life and Lore).

10 9 8 7

Sláinte!

'In my young days, when two or three men went in for a drink together, it was the custom for them to go into a back room — a snug. They never stood at the counter. Each of them would strike three hefty blows on the table and, in a flash, the barmaid would be in to see what they wanted. She would be ordered to bring them a half-pint of whiskey and, in due course, she would return with a jug and a glass. Should there be ten men in the company, they would still only have the one glass. The man who had ordered and paid for the drink would then stand up and hand a glass of whiskey to the man nearest to him, who would then say 'Here's health' (*Seo do shláinte*) to which the first man might answer, 'God grant you health' (*Sláinte ó Dhia duit*). That's the kind of toast they used to drink and it was always with a blow of the ash plant that they summoned the barman or barmaid.'

NIALL O DUBHTHAIGH

May you be poor in misfortune,
Rich in blessings,
Slow to make enemies,
Quick to make friends.
But rich or poor, quick or slow,
May you know nothing
but happiness
From this day forward.

May the face of every good news
And the back of every bad news
Be towards us.

Like the goodness of the five
loaves and two fishes,
Which God divided among the five
thousand men,
May the blessing of the King
who so divided
Be upon our share of this
common meal!

May the road rise to meet you
May the wind be always
at your back
The sun shine warm upon your face
The rain fall soft upon your fields
And until we meet again
May God hold you in the hollow
of His hand.

May the roof above us never fall in,
And may we friends gathered below
Never fall out.

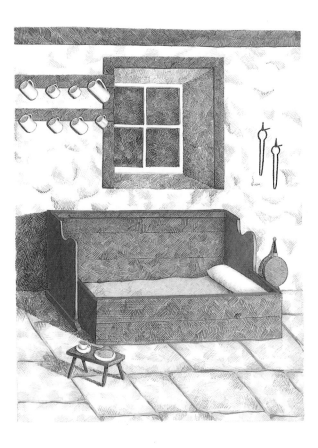

May you have food and raiment,
   A soft pillow for your head,
May you be forty years in heaven
Before the devil knows you're dead!

The health of all Ireland
and of County Mayo,
And when that much is dead,
may we still be on the go;
From the County of Meath,
the health of the hag,
Not of her but her drink
is the reason we brag;
Your health one and all,
from one wall to the other,
And, you outside there —
speak up, brother!

May the strength of three
be in your journey.

May peace and plenty be the first
To lift the latch on your door,
And happiness be guided
to your home
By the candle of Christmas.

In the New Year, may your right
hand always
Be stretched out in friendship
and never in want.

St Patrick was a gentleman
Who through strategy and stealth
Drove all the snakes from Ireland,
Here's a toasting to his health;
But not too many toastings
Lest you lose yourself and then
Forget the good St Patrick
And see all those snakes again.

May there be a fox on your
fishing-hook
And a hare on your bait
And may you kill no fish
Until St Brigid's Day.

The health of the salmon
and of the trout
That swim back and forward near
the Bull's Mouth;
Don't ask for saucepan, jug or mug,
Down the hatch — drink it up!

Here's to you and yours
and to mine and ours,
And if mine and ours ever come
across you and yours,
I hope you and yours will do
as much for mine and ours,
As mine and ours have done
for you and yours!

May you have warm words
on a cold evening,
A full moon on a dark night,
And the road downhill all the way
to your door.

May there be a generation
of children
On the children of your children.

Here's that we may always have
A clean shirt
A clean conscience
And a guinea in our pocket.

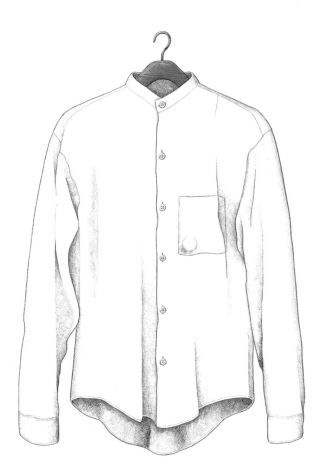

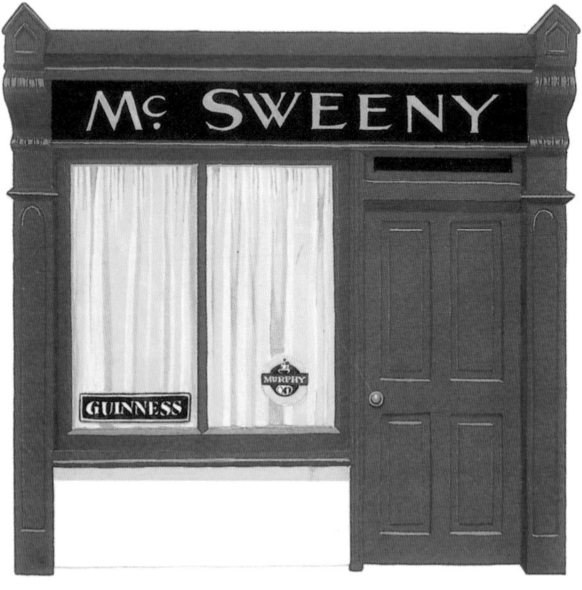
Mc SWEENY
GUINNESS
MURPHY

Here's a health
To your enemies' enemies!

Here's health and prosperity,
To you and all your posterity,
And them that doesn't drink
with sincerity,
That they may be damned
for all eternity!

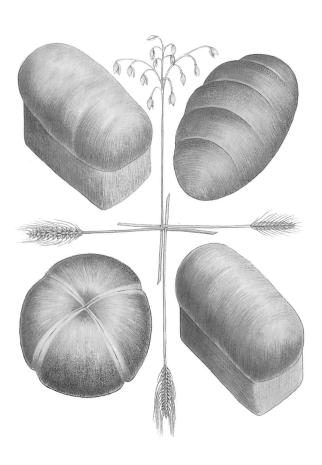

Rye bread will do you good,
Barley bread will do you no harm,
Wheaten bread will sweeten
your blood,
Oaten bread will strengthen
your arm.

May you live to be
a hundred years,
With one extra year to repent.

May I see you grey
And combing your children's hair.

Health and long life to you
The woman of your choice to you
A child every year to you
Land without rent to you
And may you die in Ireland.

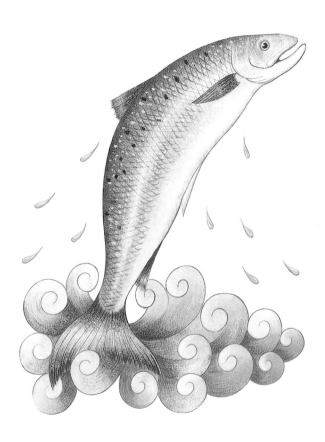

The health of the salmon to you,
A long life,
A full heart
And a wet mouth.

May the grass grow long
On the road to hell
For want of use.

May the Lord keep you
in His hand
And never close His fist too tight
on you.

Saint Brigid's Prayer

from the Irish

I'd like to give a lake of beer to God.
I'd love the Heavenly
Host to be tippling there
For all eternity.

I'd love the men of Heaven to live with me,
To dance and sing.
If they wanted, I'd put at their disposal
Vats of suffering.

White cups of love I'd give them
With a heart and a half;
Sweet pitchers of mercy I'd offer
To every man.

I'd make Heaven a cheerful spot
Because the happy heart is true.
I'd make the men contented for their own sake.
I'd like Jesus to love me too.

I'd like the people of Heaven to gather
From all the parishes around.
I'd give a special welcome to the women,
The three Marys of great renown.

I'd sit with the men, the women and God
There by the lake of beer.
We'd be drinking good health forever
And every drop would be a prayer.

BRENDAN KENNELLY